For all the grandmas and their grandchildren everywhere,
and especially for Alice xx

My Grandma

Written by Sylvia Wells
Illustrated by Sylvia Wells

Copyright © 2025 Sylvia Wells

All rights reserved. No part of this book may be reproduced in any manner whatsoever without prior written permission of the publisher.

First Printing, 2025

Published by Sylvia Wells
www.sylviawellsart.com

ISBN 978-1-7636131-1-9

My Grandma

Ruby calls her grandma "Grandma". Ruby's grandma is a painter who also makes pretty jewellery. Ruby and her grandma like to walk along the beach together.

Charlie calls his grandma "Garminy".
Garminy is a public servant who works every day on her computer. At home, Garminy likes to lift weights.
Garminy and Charlie like to go camping together.

Alice calls her grandma "Mimi".
Mimi grows beautiful flowers
and delicious fruit.
When Alice visits, they like to take
the dogs for a walk.

Abdul's grandma is called "Ayeeyo".
Ayeeyo likes to knit.
Ayeeyo works as a nurse in an aged care home.
Abdul likes to listen to Ayeeyo's stories.

Louis' grandma is called "Grandmère". Grandmère volunteers, helping new refugees with their language skills. Grandmère and Louis love to go to the park together.

Wei's grandma is called "Laolao".
Laolao works at the supermarket and helps Wei's mum look after baby Yung. Laolao lives with Wei's family and they like to cook dumplings together.

Sarah keeps a picture of her grandma who she calls "Nanna".
Nanna died before Sarah was born. Sarah's mum says that Sarah looks like her nanna.
Nanna used to play the guitar and sing.
Sarah likes singing too.

Olivia calls her grandma, "Nonna".
Nonna writes books. Olivia loves it when her nonna helps Olivia build castles with the sofa and they play games together.

Jose calls his grandma, "Abuela". Abuela makes beautiful pottery pots and cups that she sells at the market. The last time when Jose saw Abuela, they played soccer together.

Jude's grandma is called "Katie-ma". Katie-ma is a social worker. When Jude visits Katie-ma, they like to work on puzzles together.

Theo calls his grandma, "Yiayia".
Yiayia has a small farm with dairy goats and chickens.
Together, Theo and Yiayia like to play loud music and dance.

Eli calls his grandma, "Oma". Oma teaches at a primary school and has 3 cats. Eli and Oma like to read books together.

My grandma's name is..
I call her..
My grandma works/used to work as a.................
....
My grandma and I like to ....
....
Other things about my grandma.........................
....
....
....
....
....
....
....

Place a photo or a picture
of your grandma and you
on this page.

About Sylvia Wells:
Sylvia Wells lives in southern Tasmania with her husband, two youngest boys, two dogs and several pet goats.
Sylvia is very blessed to be a grandma!
Sylvia loves special time with her family, writing and reading books, painting watercolour, making things, time with her animals and in her garden.
'My Grandma' is Sylvia's 2nd children's picture book.
Her first book, 'George's Tiger' was published in 2024.

www.ingramcontent.com/pod-product-compliance
Lightning Source LLC
Chambersburg PA
CBHW041704160426
43209CB00017B/1739